Brad Roe's journey as a chef has taken him to various five-star hotels in cities such as London, Orlando, LA and Las Vegas. He also writes vegan recipes for two magazines – Britain's top selling Vegan Food and Living as well as the USA based Vegworld online magazine.
www.bradroechef.com
Instagram – bradroechef. Twitter - @bradroechef

BRAD ROE

PLANT

BASED COOKBOOK

Simple vegan cooking with a gourmet twist

This book is dedicated to anyone who has decided to enter a plant-based diet, whether that be for health, environmental or even political reasons. It is also intended for many chefs out there, that are learning the new vegan diet.

Not only is it a big step for someone to make such a drastic change in their daily diet but it is also an eye-opening journey for the cooking side of it. Even trained and well skilled chefs are beginning to learn the new challenges of creating a well-balanced vegan menu.

I started plant-based cooking ten years ago as we had to feed Garth Brooks on numerous occasions, at the Encore hotel in Las Vegas where he was performing. A six-course vegan menu which was certainly a quick way of learning the plant based way of cooking! Here is a collection of some of my recipes over the years and I hope to inspire and make your daily cooking session at home more of an event rather than a daily chore!

One of the reasons why I decided to write a vegan cookbook was to help you take the headache out of plant-based cooking. there are many chefs out there who have that fear factor of when a vegan walks into a restaurant! "I had it also ten years ago". Now, they could pop my book on a shelf in their kitchen and I would like to believe, that I could help them in some way feed their guests. Also, if you have any questions or concerns, feel free to contact me on…

Some of the recipes in this book have been made using local products made on the Isle of Wight. For such a small island, we are extremely fortunate to have some amazing produce made and grown here. Below are some of those ingredients used in this book as well as other unique items I have found along my journey.

Tipsy wight - page 5 & 52 tipsywight.com. Isle of Wight tomatoes – page 5, 13 & 51 thetomatostall.co.uk. Wight salt – page 8 & 23 wightsalt.co.uk. Ventnor botanic ale - page 29 botanic.co.uk. Mermaid Gin - page 59 isleofwightdistillery.com. Wild Mushrooms - page 34 iwmushrooms.co.uk Oil of Wight - page 7 & 40 oilofwight.co.uk Island tea leaf – page 60 islandroasted.co.uk Artisanal Bread - page 40 cantinaventnor.co.uk Maldon smoked sea salt – pages 6 & 17 maldonsalt.com Cactus & Huitlacoche "corn truffle"- page 12 mexgrocer.com
12 year aged Aceto balsamico di Modena – page 8 modenaestense.com

Other books by Brad Roe – From Cook to Chef – "Recipes and culinary tips into the chef world" https://www.amazon.co.uk/dp/1661264875.

RECIPES

KOHLRABI BRAISED IN TIPSY WIGHT CHILLI VODKA

What you need
For the kohlrabi

1 kohlrabi, peeled and cut into 1inch thick slices
20g sage leaves, finely chopped
0.5 teaspoon ground sea salt
0.5 teaspoon black onion seeds
250ml water
200ml bottle of tipsy wight chilli vodka

What you do
1. Preheating your oven to 200°c/400°f.
1. Place the kohlrabi slices into a roasting pan and add the rest of the ingredients, putting the onion seeds onto each slice of kohlrabi. Cover with foil and bake for 30 minutes or until tender.

TRIO OF CANAPES

Butternut squash & isle of wight tomato with crispy olive

What you need
4 tortillas, cut into 2inch discs – fried till crispy

1 butternut squash, cut in half and deseeded
2 Isle of wight tomatoes, one red, one yellow
One handful of kalamata olives, roughly chopped

What you do

1. Dehydrate the olives in a dehydrator overnight then cut into a coarse powder. If you do not have a dehydrator, bake them in your oven at 110°c/230°f for 3 hours, let cool then cut into a coarse powder.
2. Lay the squash onto a baking tray cut side up, drizzle with olive oil and a touch of sea salt and black pepper, bake at 180°c/350°f for 30 minutes, take out the flesh from the skin, then mash up with a potato masher. Assemble the squash on top of the disc, then 2 slices of tomatoes followed by a sprinkling of olive powder.

Guacamole with pumpkin relish

What you need

2 avocados, seeded
40g coriander, leaves picked off the stem
Juice of half a lemon
2 tablespoons pumpkin relish, page 63. Plus 1 teaspoon of Maldon smoked sea salt.

What you do

1. Mash up the avocados then add the coriander and lemon. Season with a touch of ground sea salt and ground black pepper.
2. Place the guacamole onto a fried tortilla disc followed by a teaspoon of the pumpkin relish. Sprinkle with the smoked Maldon sea salt.

LEMONGRASS POACHED CISTUS

What you need

1 Kohlrabi, peeled and sliced into 2inch discs, 3mm thick
1 Celeriac, peeled and sliced into 2inch discs, 3mm thick
1 Potato, peeled and sliced into 2inch discs, 3mm thick
2 large turnips, peeled and sliced into 2inch discs, 3mm thick

9 Cistus leaves

1 stick of lemongrass, cut into 1inch pieces

2 tablespoons oil of wight

What you do

1. To make 3 cistus towers, first start out by preheating the oven to 180°c/350°f.
2. Lay out the potatoes, kohlrabi, celeriac and lemongrass into a large roasting pan. Just barely cover with water then cover with foil.
3. Bake for 20 minutes, take off the foil and start arranging the towers. One layer of celeriac for the base, followed by a cistus leaf then a layer of potato, then cistus leaf, then a layer of kohlrabi followed by a cistus leaf, then top off with a layer of turnip.
4. Drizzle the oil of wight over the kohlrabi and serve as a canape or an accompaniment.

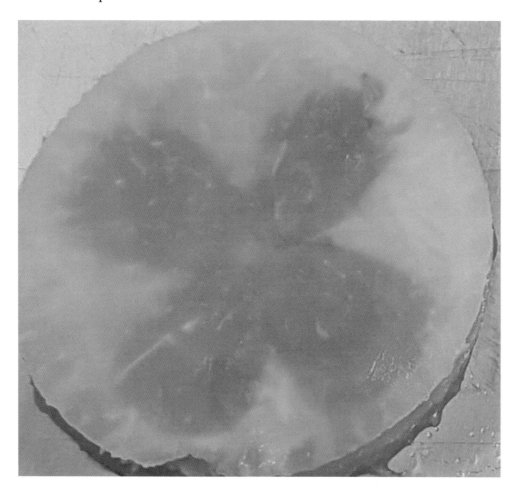

ROASTED TOMATO SALAD

What you need

12 cherry tomatoes
2 red bell pepper, sliced
3 tablespoons red onions, finely sliced
2 tablespoons pine nuts, toasted
100g mizuna or rocket lettuce
1 lemon, juiced
150ml balsamic vinegar
2 tablespoons extra virgin olive oil
3 tablespoons shaved cauliflower

What you do

1. Preheat your oven to 200°c/400°f then using a large roasting pan, add the tomatoes, peppers, balsamic vinegar and olive oil. Season with the wight salt and black pepper then roast for 30 minutes or until they are blackened and blistered.
2. In a medium sized bowl, add the lettuce, onions, pine nuts, lemon juice and cauliflower. Mix well then place onto a platter, dress with the roasted tomato and pepper mixture as well as any remaining juices in the pan.

ISLE OF WIGHT TOMATO NUT ROAST

What you need

200g Isle of Wight tomatoes, sliced
1 tablespoon pumpkin seeds
1 tablespoon sunflower seeds
5 shallots, peeled and finely chopped
100g barley
300ml vegetable stock
2 tablespoons linseed
1 large, sweet potato, peeled and finely chopped
1 tablespoon coconut oil
4 cloves garlic, peeled and finely chopped
1 tablespoon finely chopped rosemary
1 teaspoon Maldon smoked sea salt

What you do

1. Using a medium sized skillet on medium heat, add a splash of olive oil. When the oil is hot, add the shallots and garlic, when the garlic starts to brown, add the barley, linseed, coconut oil, sweet potato and vegetable stock.
2. Bring to a boil then simmer for 35 minutes, take off the heat and let cool slightly.
3. Using a metal mould ring or loaf tin, pack in the barley mixture then arrange the sliced tomatoes on top followed by a sprinkling of rosemary and the seeds. Drizzle with a splash of olive oil then bake for 10 minutes at 200°c/400°f.

PINE NUT CORNBREAD

What you need

For the cornbread
60g pine nuts, toasted
230ml coconut oil, melted
300ml almond milk
430g cornmeal
100g plain flour
1 teaspoon baking powder
½ teaspoon baking soda
Pinch of ground sea salt & black pepper

For the sweet potato puree
1 medium sized sweet potato, cut into 2inch chunks
4 tablespoons soy milk

For the sun-dried tomato cream
80g sun dried tomatoes
2 shallots, roughly chopped
8 basil leaves
470ml almond milk
1 pak choi
4 tablespoons rapeseed oil

For the tomato salad
10 cherry tomatoes, cut into quarters
50g chives, finely chopped
Juice of half a lemon

What you do

For the cornbread
1. Preheat your oven to 200°c/400°f then in a medium sized bowl mix the flour, pine nuts, cornmeal, baking powder, baking soda, salt and pepper together.
2. Using a separate bowl, mix the coconut oil & almond milk then add this to the cornmeal mixture and thoroughly mix. Grease a 9-inch square baking tin with

olive oil (or use 6 mini moulds) fill with the mixture then bake for 30 minutes. If you insert a knife into the cornbread, pull it out the check to see if the knife is clean and hot then it is ready.

For the sweet potato puree
Place the sweet potatoes into a pot, cover with water and boil for 25 minutes or until soft, drain then add the soy milk and mash up. Season to taste.

For the sun-dried tomato cream
1. Place all the ingredients into a medium sized saucepan, bring to a boil then simmer for 20 minutes.
2. Puree in a standing blender on high speed for 40 seconds then season to taste.

For the pak choi
1. Using a large sauté pan on medium heat add the rapeseed oil. When the oil is hot, add 4 pak choi leaves. Cook for 10 seconds then turn over and continue cooking for another 10 seconds.
2. Place onto a baking tray, cover with parchment paper and another tray on top to weigh the leaves down. Bake at 200°c/400°f for 1 hour. Leave to cool down then carefully take off the paper.

HUITLACOCHE TOSTADA WITH CACTUS SALSA

What you need

4 6inch blue corn tortillas "or plain tortillas"
400g huitlacoche
200g vegan cheese
2 corn on the cobs
200g cactus strips
1 yellow pepper, roughly diced
2 tomatoes, roughly diced
1 jalapeno, finely chopped
Juice of 1 lemon
40g coriander, roughly chopped

What you do

1. Using a large skillet, fry the tortillas in a touch of olive oil, fry on both sides for roughly 1 minute or until crispy. Drain onto paper towels.
2. Using a griddle pan on high heat, add the corn on the cob and cactus strips. Thoroughly char these 2 items until of a dark char all over, leave to cool then cut the kernels off the cob and cut the cactus into 1cm pieces.
3. Into a small bowl, mix the yellow pepper, cactus, lemon juice, jalapeno, tomatoes & coriander and season to taste with a touch of sea salt and ground black pepper.
4. Using a large sauté pan on high heat, add a splash of olive oil, then cook the huitlacoche for 2 minutes, season with a touch of sea salt and black pepper and arrange the huitlacoche onto each tortilla followed by the charred corn, then crumble up the vegan cheese on top. Bake in the oven for 3 minutes then place onto a serving plate with the cactus salsa on top of the tostadas.

LENTIL & HERITAGE TOMATO CHILLI

What you need

For the chilli
1 medium sized red onion, peeled & roughly chopped
12 large tomatoes, such as beef steak from Isle of Wight tomatoes, cored & cut in half
250g yellow lentils
400g tin kidney beans
1 red pepper, roughly chopped
1 yellow pepper, roughly chopped

1 jalapeno, finely chopped
1 tbsp smoked paprika
2 tsp ground cumin
2 tsp ground coriander
1 tbsp tomato puree
2 litres vegetable stock
3 tbsp balsamic vinegar
2 tbsp olive oil
5 cloves garlic, peeled & finely chopped
1 tbsp rosemary, finely chopped
200ml red wine

For the bread bowl
1.5 litre warm water
21g easy bake yeast
½ tsp ground sea salt
1kilo rye flour
500g granary flour
3 Tbsp black treacle

What you do

Rye bread bowl
1. Using a medium sized bowl, add both flours and mix in the yeast and salt.
2. In a separate small bowl stir in the black treacle with the water until its combined then add this to the rye flour mix, beat the mixture for roughly 8 minutes in which it should be of a sticky texture.
3. Place the dough mix onto a table with a generous dusting of rye flour then form into 4 dough balls. Cover loosely with some cling film then leave to prove in a slightly warm area for 50 minutes.
4. Preheat your oven to 180°c/350°f, place the dough ball onto a baking tray lined with greased parchment paper. Bake for 1 hour then leave to cool. Cut of the top part of the bread and reserve for the lid, then cut out the inner bread to make room for the chilli.

For the red lentil & tomato chilli
1. Start off by roasting your tomatoes. Place them onto a baking tray skin side down, drizzle with 1 tbsp of the olive oil and the 3 tbsp of balsamic vinegar. Bake for 30 minutes at 200°c/400°c then set aside to cool. When ok

to handle, give them a rough chop keeping any of the lovely juices "roasting the tomatoes helps to concentrate the flavour".

2. Using a medium sized pot on medium heat, add a splash of olive oil then add the onions and both peppers. When the onions start to brown, add the ground cumin, coriander and smoked paprika, thoroughly mix in for roughly 20 seconds.

3. Add the remaining ingredients including the cooked tomatoes, bring to a boil then simmer for 1 hour. Season to taste then spoon into the warmed bread bowls.

*Chefs note.

- Any next day leftovers, add a splash of soy milk to the heated chilli, then puree for a nice creamy lentil soup.
- Tomatoes were first cultivated by the ancient Aztecs in 700 AD. The actual name tomato comes from the Nahuatl word "tomatl" which translates as "fat water"!

ASPARAGUS & ROASTED PEPPER SALAD

What you need

1 red bell pepper
1 yellow bell pepper
6 stalks of asparagus, cut into ½ inch pieces
200g cherry or heritage tomatoes, cut into bite size pieces
2 tablespoons balsamic vinegar, such as Malpighi
12 thin slices of peeled watermelon radish
1 tablespoon pine nuts, toasted
½ teaspoon black onion seeds
1 teaspoon extra virgin olive oil

What you do

1. Start off by roasting your peppers over a naked flame, simply place the peppers on your burners and blacken all over until thoroughly blackened and blistered.
2. Put them into a bowl then cover with cling film, let sit for 10 minutes then peel the skin and deseed.
3. Cut the peppers into thin strips then set aside.
4. Grill the asparagus on a chargrill until you have nice dark grilled marks on them, then add these to the peppers.
5. Combine the rest of the ingredients to the pepper mix and gently mix the salad.

KOHLRABI TACOS WITH CHICKPEA PUREE, SALSA VERDE & PEA SHOOTS

What you need

For the chickpea puree

1 tablespoon smoked paprika
8 sprigs thyme
1 tablespoon olive oil
1 kohlrabi, sliced on mandolin into 2mm thick slices, or as thin as you can cut them.
7oz raw chickpeas
4 bay leaves
1½ litre vegetable stock
20g pea shoots - for garnish
1 lime, juiced

For the salsa verde

1 red onion, peeled and cut into quarters
10 tomatillos, husks removed and cut in half
6 cloves garlic, peeled
2 jalapenos, stems discarded & cut in half lengthwise
Juice of half a lemon
30g cilantro

What you do

Chickpea puree

1. In a medium sized pot on medium heat, add the vegetable stock, bay leaves, smoked paprika & chickpeas. Cover & simmer for roughly 80 minutes or until the peas are cooked but still have a slight bite to them. Towards the end of cooking, add water if the stock reduces too much.
2. Strain the chickpeas, add a splash of olive oil then give them a little mash up with a masher. Add the lime juice & season to taste.

Salsa verde

1. Place all the ingredients apart from the lemon juice and cilantro into a roasting pan with parchment paper, drizzle with a slight touch of olive oil then roast in the oven at 200°c/400°f for roughly 35 minutes or until all the vegetables are charred and blistered. They should be slightly blackened.
2. Add the lemon juice and cilantro, blend with a food processor for roughly 4 seconds then scrape down the edges then blend again for a further 4 seconds "it's nice to have a slight coarse texture to it". Season to taste with sea salt & black pepper.

To assemble the tacos - spread the chickpea puree onto a kohlrabi disc
followed by the salsa then the pea shoots.

FONDANT TURNIP & ASPARAGUS TAQUITO'S

What you need

For the chilli salt
4 jalapeno chillies
200g Maldon smoked sea salt

For the taquitos
1 medium sized turnip, peeled and cut into roughly 1cm cubes
3 tablespoons vegan butter
1 bunch asparagus, cut into ¼ pieces
1 medium sized red onion, peeled and roughly chopped
1 tablespoon sage, finely chopped
150g chipotle peppers in adobo sauce, pureed
200g grated vegan cheese
12 corn tortillas
300ml vegetable stock

For the taquito sauce
200g chipotle peppers in adobe sauce, pureed
200ml oat milk
150g grated vegan cheese

What you do

For the chilli salt
1. Cut the chillies in half lengthwise then cut off the stem, lay out on a dehydrating tray and dehydrate overnight on the highest setting. If you do not have an oven, you can dehydrate the chillies in the oven for 3 hours at 110°c/230°f".
2. The chillies should now be of a firm texture, make sure they are at room temperature then place them into a spice grinder or mortar and pestle along with the Maldon sea salt. Grind until you have a powdery substance and set aside.

For the taquitos

1. Preheat your oven to 350°f/180°c. Using a medium sized roasting pan, add the turnips, onion and vegetable stock. Cover with foil then bake for 30 minutes, take out of the oven then add the asparagus, chipotle and sage. Continue to cook for another 7 minutes.
2. Lay out the tortillas and place 2 tablespoons of the vegetable filling onto the bottom of each tortilla followed by a sprinkle of chilli salt and the vegan cheese. Roll up to the top of each one then secure with a toothpick. Place them onto a large baking tray, drizzle with olive oil then bake for 8 minutes at 190°c/375°f or until the taquitos ends are golden brown.
3. Leave to cool slightly so you can take out the toothpicks. Take the taquitos and place into a large baking dish, mix the oat milk and chipotle sauce together then pour over the taquitos. Sprinkle over the grated cheese along with a drizzle of olive oil to help the cheese melt. Bake at 180°c/350°f for 15 minutes or until the cheese is golden brown.

JACKFRUIT SWEET CHILLI NOODLES

What you need

1 12oz tin jackfruit, drained
1 yellow bell pepper, thinly sliced
1 red bell pepper, thinly sliced
2 shallots, peeled and thinly sliced
100ml white wine
400g udon noodles
200ml sweet chilli sauce
30g coriander leaf, roughly chopped
1 lime, juiced

What you do

1. Blanch your noodles by boiling them in salted water for 2 minutes then drain.
2. In a medium sized sauté pan, add the wine, onions & peppers. Simmer until the wine has almost evaporated then toss in the rest of the ingredients. When boiling, take off the heat and serve.

ROOT VEGETABLE SALAD WITH TARRAGON DRESSING

What you need

For the salad
1 medium sized red onion, roughly chopped
1 small turnip, cut into roughly 2cm cubes
1 small swede, cut into roughly 2cm cubes
1 medium sized carrot, cut into roughly 1cm cubes
2 medium sized parsnips, cut into roughly 1cm pieces
1 head of radicchio, cored, cut in half and leaves separated
1 head of romaine lettuce, roughly chopped

For the dressing
60g tarragon, roughly chopped
2 shallots, peeled and finely diced
2 teaspoons Dijon mustard
1 tablespoon brown sugar
1 lime, juiced
4 tablespoons apple cider vinegar
160ml rapeseed oil

What you do

For the root vegetables
Using a large roasting pan, add the red onion, turnip, swede, carrot & parsnip then mix together with a good glug of olive oil and 2 cups of water. Cover with foil then bake at 180°c for 20 minutes, take off the foil then bake for a further 20 minutes, set aside.

For the radicchio
Using a char grill, slightly drizzle with olive oil then char the radicchio leaves until thoroughly charred on both sides then set aside.

For the dressing

Place the shallots, mustard, vinegar, tarragon, sugar and lime into a standing blender, blend on medium speed for 10 seconds then drizzle in the rapeseed oil in a steady stream.

Season to taste with ground sea salt and ground black pepper.

CARDAMON CRUSTED CAULIFLOWER WITH PICO DE GALLO

What you need

For the cauliflower

1 tablespoon cardamom seeds
1 medium sized cauliflower, cut into one-inch slabs "with the root intact"
1 tablespoon olive oil

For the pico de gallo

4 medium sized tomatoes, cut into roughly 1cm sized cubes
4 tablespoons red onion, finely chopped
1 jalapeno, finely chopped "I keep the seeds in, feel free to take them out"
40g coriander, roughly chopped
Juice of half a lemon

What you do

For the cauliflower

1. Preheat your oven to 190°c/375°f. Using a small sauté pan, toast the cardamom seeds on medium heat just until they start to char, roughly 50 seconds. Let cool then grind in a spice grinder or mortar and pestle.
2. Using a large roasting tray lined with parchment paper, drizzle with a touch of oil and sprinkle over half the cardamom spice powder. Lay the cauliflower slabs on top then repeat with the olive oil and cardamom. Sprinkle with a touch of ground sea salt and black pepper.

3. Place into the oven and bake for 25 minutes, take out and set aside.

For the pico de gallo
Mix all the ingredients together into a bowl and season to taste with ground sea salt and black pepper. If you like your salsa spicier just add two jalapenos instead of one.

ROOT VEGETABLE LASAGNE WITH A WATERCRESS COULIS

What you need

For the lasagne
One large turnip, peeled and sliced into a ½ cm thick, 4inch rectangular slab
One large aubergine, peeled and sliced into a ½ cm thick, 4inch rectangular slab
One large swede, peeled and sliced into a ½ cm thick, 4inch rectangular slab
130g Kalamata olives, pitted and roughly chopped
20g sage, roughly chopped
Juice of one lime
1 12oz can refried beans
1 Yellow pepper
3 medium sized tomatoes, finely chopped
200g vegan grated cheese
2 tablespoons olive oil
¼ teaspoon ground sea salt
¼ teaspoon ground black pepper

For the watercress coulis
200g watercress
4 shallots, roughly chopped
Juice of half a lemon
300ml oat milk
¼ teaspoon ground sea salt
Pinch of ground black pepper

What you do

For the lasagne

1. Preheat your oven to 190°c/375°f. Using a char-gridle on a medium flame, char the turnip, swede and aubergine slices on both sides until they are thoroughly charred.
2. Mix the olives, sage and lime together and set aside.
3. Lay out the turnip slices onto a greased baking tray then add 1 tablespoon of the olive mix. Add the swede then put the refried beans & yellow peppers on top of the swede.
4. Finally, add the aubergine slice followed by the diced tomatoes. Place the vegan grated cheese on top with a little drizzle of olive oil then bake for 25 minutes.

For the watercress coulis

1. Place all the ingredients into a medium sized saucepan, bring to a boil then simmer for 30 minutes, transfer to a standing blender. Puree on high speed for 40 seconds then season to taste with ground sea salt and ground black pepper.

GOLDEN BEETROOT & KALE TOSTADA WITH SALSA RANCHERA

What you need

For the tostada

4 corn tortillas
2 large golden yellow beetroots, peeled and cut into 2cm cubes
4 shallots, peeled & roughly chopped
2 tablespoons vegan butter
400ml vegetable stock
½ teaspoon ground sea salt
1 head of kale, roughly chopped with inner thick stalks discarded

For the salsa ranchera

4 medium sized tomatoes, cored
1 small red onion, peeled and cut into 6 slices
2 jalapenos, cut in half lengthwise and stem discarded
5 cloves garlic, peeled
1 teaspoon olive oil
½ teaspoon ground sea salt
¼ teaspoon ground black pepper
50g coriander
Juice of one lemon

For the plantain chip

1 fresh plantain
2 tablespoons plain flour
2 teaspoons smoked paprika
3 tablespoons rapeseed oil

What you do

For the beetroot & kale tostada

1. Preheat your oven to 190°c/375°f. Using a large roasting tray, add the beetroot, shallots, vegetable stock, vegan butter, salt and pepper. Cover with foil then bake for 30 minutes.
2. Take out the beetroot and add the kale, stir in then cook for a further 10 minutes.
3. Place the tortillas on a baking tray, drizzle with a touch of olive oil then bake for 3 minutes to crisp up.

For the salsa ranchera

1. Using a medium sized bowl add everything apart from the coriander and lemon, drizzle with the 1 teaspoon of olive oil and toss to coat. Heat up a griddle pan and char the vegetables on a high heat until they are thoroughly charred and blackened.
2. Place the charred vegetables into a standing blender, add the coriander and lemon juice and blitz. Puree for a nice slightly chunky texture, 7-10 seconds maximum.

For the plantain chip

1. Peel the plantains then place into the freezer. When they are slightly frozen "roughly takes about 90 minutes" slice them lengthwise into 3mm slices then place onto a tray.
2. Mix the flour and paprika together in a small bowl then sprinkle this mixture over the plantain slices, using caution to not break the plantains.
3. Using a large sauté pan on medium heat, add 3 tablespoons of canola oil and fry off the plantain slices until golden brown, roughly 15 seconds on each side.
4. Take out the slices and drain onto paper towels. Season with a touch of ground sea salt.

To assemble the dish

Place the baked tortilla onto your serving plate then spread the salsa onto one half of the tortilla followed by the beetroot and kale on the other side. Garnish with the plantain chip.

KOHLRABI & ONION SEED BAHJIS

What you need

For the bahji
1 kohlrabi, peeled and finely shredded on a grater
250g red onion, peeled and very finely chopped
1 tablespoon onion seeds
1 teaspoon cumin
1 teaspoon coriander
½ teaspoon turmeric
1 jalapeno, stem discarded and finely diced
1 teaspoon smoked paprika
2 tablespoons coconut oil
3 tablespoons hummus
100g chickpea flour
4 tablespoons rice flour
100ml oat milk
1 teaspoon wight sea salt – for finishing
¼ teaspoon ground black pepper
200ml canola oil, for frying

What you do

1. Place the onions and kohlrabi into a clean towel and try to squeeze as much water out as you can. Put this mixture into a large mixing bowl then add the rest of the ingredients. Mix thoroughly with your hands, you are wanting a mixture that is still wet that slowly drops off a spoon when you hold it up. If too dry just add some more oat milk, if too wet just add some chickpea flour.
2. Wash your hands and line a tray with parchment paper, using 2 tablespoons or an ice cream scoop, spoon out the mixture individually onto the tray and place in the fridge for 30 minutes.
3. As the kohlrabi mixture is chilling, heat up the canola oil in a deep skillet to 180°c/350°f then shallow fry the bahjis for roughly 2 minutes or until they are golden brown on each side. Drain onto paper towels and sprinkle over the wight sea salt.

WATERMELON & APPLE VODKA GRANITA WITH ORANGE JALAPENO SQUASH

What you need

For the watermelon granita
1.5kilo of watermelon, peeled and cut into large chunks, discarding the seeds
30g brown sugar
1 lime, juiced

For the apple vodka granita
900g apples, cored and cut into chunks
700ml apple juice
50g brown sugar
2 teaspoons apple cider vinegar

For the orange jalapeno squash
400ml orange juice
2 jalapenos, roughly chopped

What you do

For the watermelon granita
1. Juice the watermelon in a standing blender then mix in the lime juice and sugar. Place into a medium sized pot, bring to a simmer then take off the heat. Let cool slightly then pour into a baking tray and fill the tray 2cm deep with the granita.
2. Leave to freeze for 5 hours, then use long swipes with a fork to get the shavings of granita of the tray.

For the apple vodka granita
1. Put all the items into a medium sized pan, bring to a boil then simmer until the apples are of a pulp form.
2. Place this mixture into a fine strainer and push out as much liquid as you can, this helps in thickening the granita.
3. Put the mixture onto a large baking tray and fill up to 2cm deep. Leave in the freezer for 5 hours then use long swipes with a fork to get the shavings of granita off the tray.

For the orange jalapeno squash
1. Put all the ingredients into a medium sized pot, then bring to a simmer.
2. Simmer for 1 minute then take off the heat, strain through a muslin cloth then leave to cool in the fridge.

ROOT VEGETABLE MEDLEY, SWEET CORN CREAM & CRISPY KALE LEAF

What you need

For the vegetable medley
1 medium sized beetroot, peeled and cut into 2cm chunks
2 heritage carrots, peeled and cut into 2cm chunks
2 parsnips, peeled and cut into 2cm chunks
1 celeriac, peeled and cut into 2cm chunks

1 kohlrabi, peeled and cut into 2cm chunks
4 shallots, peeled and roughly chopped
1 sprig rosemary, roughly chopped
2 sprigs tarragon, roughly chopped
4 tablespoons vegan butter
250ml vegetable stock

For the sweetcorn cream
1 corn on the cob, corn cut off the cob, keep the cob
3 shallots, peeled and roughly chopped
60g cashew nuts, roasted
300ml almond milk

For the crispy kale leaf
1 whole kale, 4 whole leaves separated
3 tablespoons canola oil
Pinch of ground sea salt

What you do

For the crispy kale leaf
1. Using a large skillet, add the canola oil and heat to 180°c/350°f. Fry the leaves on each side for 12 seconds. Drain onto a baking tray lined with parchment paper and season with the sea salt.
2. Add another piece of parchment paper on top then rest another baking tray on top to weigh down the leaf "this helps flatten the leaf and to dehydrate evenly". Bake in the oven for 3 hours at 80°c/180°f. Carefully take off the paper and handle the leaf gently as it should be crisp to the touch.

For the sweetcorn cream
1. Using a large skillet, add a splash of olive oil then add the shallots and sweetcorn plus cob.
2. When the shallots start to brown, add the almond milk and cashew nuts, simmer for 20 minutes. Puree in a standing blender on high speed for 1 minute.

For the roasted vegetables

1. Preheat your oven to 180°c/350°f. Using a large deep roasting pan, add the carrots, beetroot, vegan butter, a big pinch of sea salt and the vegetable stock. Cover with foil and bake for 20 minutes.
2. Take the roasting pan out of the oven and add the celeriac, kohlrabi, shallots, rosemary and tarragon. Mix in then cover with the foil, bake for a further 25 minutes or until the vegetables are cooked but still have a slight firmness to them. Season to taste with ground sea salt and black pepper.

To assemble the dish

Using a ladle, put the sweetcorn cream into the centre of the plate, roasted vegetables on top then garnish with the kale leaf.

CHARRED VEGETABLE LASAGNE WITH SWEET POTATO CREAM

What you need

For the vegetable lasagne
1 small celeriac, peeled and sliced into ½ cm thick slices
1 swede, peeled and sliced into ½ cm thick slices
1 medium sized eggplant, sliced into 1cm thick slices
12 green olives, pitted and finely diced
50g tarragon, finely chopped
200g vegan cheese, shredded

For the sweet potato cream
1 sweet potato, peeled and cut into 1inch pieces
300ml almond milk, heated

What you do

For the vegetable lasagne
1. Using a 4-5inch rectangular mould cutter, cut the celeriac, swede & eggplant into rectangular slabs, season with a little sea salt and black pepper and drizzle with a little olive oil.

2. Using a char-grill or BBQ, grill the celeriac and swede on both sides to obtain dark grill marks and set aside. Place the eggplant onto a baking tray, then stack the swede on top then the celeriac, cover with foil then bake at 175°c/350°f for 25 minutes.

3. Discard the foil, mix the olives and tarragon and arrange neatly on top of the lasagne. Dress with the cheese then pop back in the oven to melt the cheese for roughly 4 minutes.

For the sweet potato cream

1. Using a medium sized saucepan, cover the sweet potato with water and boil until thoroughly cooked, roughly 20 minutes.

2. Strain the potato then add to a standing blender, gradually add the almond milk and blend on high speed until thoroughly combined, the sauce should coat the back of a spoon, if not, just add some more almond milk then season to taste with sea salt and black pepper. If the sauce is too thin, just reduce it in a pot on the stove.

PINE NUT CORNBREAD

What you need

For the cornbread
60g pine nuts, toasted
230ml coconut oil
400ml almond milk
150g cornmeal
80g all-purpose flour
1 teaspoon baking powder
¼ teaspoon baking soda

For the sweet potato puree
1 sweet potato, peeled and cut into 1inch
pieces 300ml vegetable stock
½ tablespoon olive oil

For the sweetcorn cream
One corn on the cob, kernels cut off and keep the cob
4 shallots, peeled and roughly chopped
400ml almond milk

For the garnish
Two raw chard leaves

What you do

For the pine nut cornbread
1. In a large bowl, mix the flour, pine nuts, cornmeal, baking powder, baking soda and sea salt.
2. Using another bowl, mix the coconut oil & almond milk, add this mixture to the cornmeal mix and thoroughly combine.
3. Grease an 8inch baking dish "or individual moulds" with a little butter then pour the cornbread mixture in, bake at 200°c/400°f for 22 minutes, check with a toothpick or knife, if it comes out clean and hot then its ready.

For the sweet potato puree

1. Place the sweet potatoes onto a baking tray along with the vegetable stock, olive oil, honey and a touch of sea salt and black pepper. Cover the tray with foil.

2. Bake at 175°c/350°f for 30 minutes or until the liquid has evaporated and you can easily put a knife through one.

3. Place into a bowl then mash together for a rustic chunky & funky mash.

For the sweet corn cream

1. Using a medium sized sauté pan on medium heat, add the olive oil, sweetcorn, the cob and the shallots. Cook on medium heat for 2 minutes then add the almond milk.

2. Simmer for 20 minutes then discard the cob.

3. Puree the sauce then pass through a strainer to remove any skins of corn.

Garnish

1. Using a medium sized skillet on medium heat, add the olive oil, then add the chard leaf, fry on both sides for only 13 seconds.

2. Place the chard leaf onto a baking pan lined with parchment paper, sprinkle a touch of salt onto it then place another piece of paper on top. Put a tray directly on top to weigh down the leaf, this will help it set into a nice flat crispy leaf, then bake at 150°c/300°f for 25 minutes or until the leaf is crisp to the touch.

SWEDE ENCHILADAS

What you need

For the Cajun pearl barley & swede enchiladas
100g pearl barley
400ml vegetable stock
½ teaspoon sea salt
6 shallots, peeled and roughly chopped
1 small swede, peeled and cut into 1cm cubes
12oz can of chipotle peppers, roughly chopped
30g cilantro, roughly chopped
2 tablespoons Cajun spice powder
5 medium sized tomatoes, roughly chopped
2 10inch white tortilla's
125g vegan cheese, shredded

For the pea shoot coulis
400g pea shoots, trimmed and washed
500ml water
1 lime, juiced
4 shallots, peeled and roughly chopped
2 tablespoons olive oil
½ teaspoon sea salt
230ml vegetable stock

What you do

For the Cajun pearl barley & swede enchiladas
1. Start by cooking your pearl barley off in a medium sized pot with the vegetable stock and sea salt. Bring to a boil then simmer for roughly 25-30 minutes with a lid on, then strain and set aside "they should have a slight firmness to them".
2. Using a medium sized roasting pan add the shallots, chipotle peppers, Cajun spice, swede, tomatoes & cilantro. Pour in the vegetable stock and bake in the oven at 190°c/375°f for roughly 35 minutes or until the stock is almost all evaporated, mix this mixture with the pearl barley.
4. Lay out 4 tortillas and fill with the barley & swede mixture, wrap up

like a burrito by folding over the bottom part, folding the sides in then rolling up, arrange these burritos into a baking dish and set aside.

For the pea shoot coulis

1. Put all the ingredients into a medium sized sauce pot apart from the olive oil and bring to the boil, boil for 10 minutes then strain.

2. Place into a standing blender and blend on medium speed for 10 seconds then scrape down the sides of the blender with a plastic spatula, blend again on high speed for roughly 10 seconds then slowly drizzle in the olive oil.

3. Take 1 cup of this mixture and mix with ½ cup of vegetable stock, pour into the trayed-up burritos, arrange the vegan cheese on top of the burritos then bake for 15 minutes at 190°c/375°f.

4. Ladle the pea shoot coulis onto a plate, then place the enchiladas on top.

CHICKPEA BURGER WITH POBLANO CHILI & TOMATILLO SALSA

What you need

For the vegan burger
1 12oz can cooked chickpeas
6oz cooked refried beans
80g pine nuts, toasted
1 small red onion, peeled and finely chopped
4 cloves garlic, peeled and finely chopped
3 medium sized tomatoes, roughly chopped
3 tablespoons balsamic vinegar
tablespoons olive oil
30g tarragon, roughly chopped
200ml coconut oil

For the poblano chili & tomatillo salsa
4 poblano chilies
8 fresh tomatillos, husks removed and rinsed

1 small red onion, peeled and cut into quarters
6 cloves garlic, peeled
1 tablespoon olive oil
½ teaspoon sea salt
60g cilantro, roughly chopped
2 limes, juiced

What you do

For the vegan burger

1. Using a medium sized roasting pan, add the red onion, tomatoes, garlic, balsamic vinegar & olive oil. Roast in the oven at 200°c/400°f for roughly 25 minutes or until the tomatoes are blistered and charred, set aside.
2. Into a medium sized bowl, add the chickpeas, refried beans, pine nuts, coconut oil, tarragon and the roasted tomato mixture. Mash it all up together with a potato masher making sure its thoroughly mashed up, season to taste with a touch of sea salt and black pepper then mould into 6oz burger size patties, place into the fridge for at least 3 hours to help set.
3. Using a cast iron skillet or sauté pan on medium heat, sear off the burgers in a little olive oil, place the oil into the pan and when hot, carefully put in the burgers, let them be and let sit and brown for 2 minutes, if you start to move them around they will just break apart so wait for roughly 2 minutes until there is a nice dark brown colour on the bottom sides of the burgers.
4. Then using a metal spatula, carefully turn the burgers over, sear on the other side for 1 minute then place onto a baking tray with parchment paper and bake for 20 minutes at 175°c/350°f.

Poblano chili & tomatillo salsa

1. Into a large bowl, add all the ingredients apart from the lime juice & cilantro and mix well to coat the vegetables in the oil.

2. Preferably using a barbecue or char grill, char the ingredients until nicely charred all over and almost blackened. Take off the grill and set the chilies aside into a bowl and wrap with plastic wrap, leave for 10 minutes then peel and deseed.

3. Using a standing blender, puree all the ingredients on medium speed whilst adding the cilantro and lime juice. Season to taste with sea salt and black pepper.

LOTUS ROOT RICE SALAD WITH BALSAMIC ONIONS

What you need

For the lotus root rice salad
20g lotus root, sliced into 1cm thick slices
40g basmati rice
10 mint leaves, sliced thinly
2 heritage tomatoes, cut into a small dice
1 spring onion, sliced very thinly on the bias
1 tablespoon pumpkin seeds
1 lime, juiced
1 tablespoon extra-virgin olive oil

For the kohlrabi
1 small kohlrabi, peeled & cut into 2cm cubes
20g mixed salad leaves
1 tablespoon sunflower seeds
1 tablespoon pumpkin seeds
½ teaspoon black onion seeds
one red bell pepper, cut into a small dice
6 green olives
2 tablespoons extra virgin olive oil

For the balsamic onions
Two red onions, cut into a small dice
1 tablespoon olive oil
1 tablespoon vegan butter
1 tablespoon white sugar
0.5 cup balsamic vinegar

What you do

For the lotus root
1. Place a 10inch square piece of foil onto a tray, drizzle with olive oil, lay the lotus root slices on top followed by another drizzle of olive oil and a

sprinkle of sea salt and black pepper.

2. Wrap up the package into a tight bundle then bake for 30 minutes in the oven at 200°c/400°f.

3. Take out of the oven and set aside.

For the rice salad

1. Using a small pot, fill halfway and bring to a boil, add ¼ teaspoon of salt and then the rice & give it a stir.

2. Put the lid on and let the rice cook for roughly 14 minutes, stirring a couple of times throughout cooking. Once cooked, rinse under cold water to cool. Mix with the rest of the ingredients and set aside.

For the kohlrabi salad

1. In a medium sized bowl, add the kohlrabi, a drizzle of olive oil, a knob of butter and a touch of sea salt and black pepper.

2. Toss well together and place on a baking pan lined with parchment paper. Roast at 175°c/350°f for roughly 35 minutes, giving them a stir halfway through cooking.

3. Place the kohlrabi back in a bowl and mix in the rest of the ingredients, season to taste with sea salt and black pepper.

For the balsamic onions

1. Using a medium sized pot on low heat, add the olive oil & butter, when nice and hot, add the rest of the ingredients. Turn down to a low heat and simmer for roughly 1 hour or until the relish is of a nice thick "jammy like" consistency.

ROOT VEGETABLE MADRAS CURRY WITH CUMIN BASMATI

What you need

For the root vegetable madras curry
1 small red onion, roughly chopped
200g swede, peeled and cut into roughly 1cm cubes
200g parsnips, peeled and cut into roughly 1 cm cubes
200g carrots, peeled and cut into roughly 1cm cubes
200g celeriac, peeled and cut into roughly 1cm cubes
½ teaspoon cumin seeds
1 teaspoon cardamom pods
½ teaspoon coriander seeds
1 thumb size piece of ginger, peeled & minced
4 garlic cloves, peeled and finely chopped
3 jalapeno chilies, stems discarded and finely chopped
½ teaspoon turmeric powder
1 teaspoon garam masala powder
7oz tomato puree
300ml vegetable stock or water

For the cumin scented basmati
1 cup basmati rice, rinsed
8 cups water
½ teaspoon ground sea salt
½ teaspoon cumin powder

What you do

For the root vegetable madras curry
1. Using a large sauté pan on medium heat, add the cumin, cardamom and coriander seeds, toast for roughly 1minute or until they are slightly browned, leave to cool then grind in a spice grinder or mortar and pestle then setaside.
2. Using the same pan on medium heat, add a good glug of olive oil and a knob of butter. Add the onions and carrots and cook until they are slightly browned then add the garlic. When the garlic starts to brown add the cumin, cardamom, coriander, turmeric & garam masala.

2. Mix all together and let cook for 1 minute then add the stock, ginger, vegetables, tomato puree & jalapeno. Cover with a lid then simmer for 30 minutes. Season to taste with ground sea salt and freshly ground black pepper.

For the cumin scented basmati

1. Using a medium sized pot, add the water and salt. Bring to a boil then add the basmati rice.

2. Simmer the rice with a lid on for roughly 16 minutes or until the rice is slightly tender and cooked. Strain then add the cumin, mix well and add ground sea salt if needed.

CURRIED SALSIFY WITH CRISPY OLIVES

What you need

For the salsify curry
1 tablespoon olive oil
2 coconut oil
700g salsify stalks
Half of 1 lemon
1 small red onion, roughly chopped
1 yellow pepper, deseeded and roughly chopped
5 cloves garlic, peeled and finely chopped
1 bunch asparagus, cut into 1cm slices
½ tablespoon cumin
½ tablespoon coriander
½ tablespoon garam masala
½ teaspoon ginger powder
1 tablespoon tomato paste
1 teaspoon onion seeds
1 jalapeno, finely chopped
1 12oz can diced tomatoes
30g cashew nuts, roughly chopped
300ml almond milk

For the basmati
50g basmati rice
100ml water
100ml elderflower cordial

For the crispy olives

80g kalamata olives, pitted and roughly chopped

What you do

For the crispy olives
1. Lay out the olives onto a dehydrating tray and dehydrate in your dehydrator overnight on your highest setting. If you do not have a dehydrator, lay them out on baking tray with parchment paper followed by another piece of parchment paper followed by a lid to weigh them down.
2. Bake at 90°c/190°f for 4 hours or until the olives are hard to the touch.
3. Let the olives cool to room temperature then place into a spice grinder, grind down to a coarse powder.

For the salsify curry
1. Prepare the salsify first by filling a large bowl with cold water and adding half a squeezed lemon. Start peeling the salsify then place them into this water "they turn brown very quickly without the water and lemon. When they are all peeled, slice them into 1cm slices.
2. Using a large saucepot, add the olive oil, coconut oil and onions. Sauté for roughly 3 minutes then add the garlic, cumin, coriander, jalapeno, onion seeds, garam masala and ginger. Cook for a further minute giving it a good stir, then add the salsify, asparagus, yellow pepper, tomato paste, tomatoes, almond milk and cashew nuts.
3. Bring to a boil then simmer for 30 minutes then season to taste with ground sea salt and ground black pepper.

For the basmati
1. Put the rice in a large bowl and cover with water, let it sit for 25 minutes.
2. Using a medium sized pot, add the 100ml water, the cordial, and salt then bring to the boil.
3. Let boil for 3 minutes, then drain the rice and add it to the pot. Cover with a tight-fitting lid, lower the heat to a simmer and let cook for 10 minutes.
4. Take off the heat and let sit with the lid on for a further 4 minutes, fluff up with a fork before serving.

PUMPKIN RISOTTO

What you need

300g arborio risotto rice
1 litre vegetable stock, hot
150ml white wine
2 tablespoon vegan butter
200g pumpkin relish, page 69

What you do

1. Using a large saucepan on medium heat, add a good splash of olive oil, one tablespoon of the vegan butter and the rice. Stir this rice for roughly 1 minute to give it a nice slight toastiness!
2. Adding the hot stock, one ladleful at a time until the rice has absorbed most of it. Keep stirring until all the stock has been used, roughly 13 minutes, then add the pumpkin relish.Take the risotto off the heat and mix in the other tablespoon of

butter. Let sit for a minute then season to taste with ground sea salt and ground black pepper.

PUMPKIN ARANCINI

What you need

For the pumpkin arancini
400g pumpkin risotto, chilled. page 32
2 cups breadcrumbs
2 tablespoons flour
200ml soy milk
200ml canola oil for shallow frying

For the Thai curried swede
1 swede, peeled and diced into 0.5cm cubes
1 tablespoon red thai curry paste
250ml cashew cream, page 66
300ml soy milk
30g sage, finely chopped

What you do

For the Thai curried swede
Add all the ingredients to a medium sized saucepan, bring to a boil then simmer
For 20 minutes or until the swede is cooked but still has a slight bite to it.

For the pumpkin arancini
1. Mould all the risotto into golf ball size balls then place into the freezer for one hour.
2. Lay out the flour, soy milk and breadcrumbs onto 3 separate plates then start breading the arancini.
3. One by one, roll the risotto balls into the flour, then soy milk then breadcrumbs, then repeat again to ensure a thorough coating.
4. Fry the arancini balls in a shallow sauté pan in the canola oil on a high heat, once they are all browned, they are ready, set aside.

BARLEY & KALE STEW WITH
VENTNOR BOTANIC PALE ALE

What you need

2 tablespoons olive oil
2 teaspoons smoked paprika
1 teaspoon cumin
4 tablespoons barley
1 white onion, roughly chopped
2 carrots, peeled & roughly chopped

3 sticks of celery, roughly chopped
1 leek, washed and roughly chopped
5 cloves garlic, thinly sliced
1 head of kale, washed, stems removed and roughly chopped
2 tablespoons tomato puree
1 tablespoon marmite
1 tablespoon rosemary, finely chopped
1 400g can borlotti beans
900ml vegetable stock
500ml Ventnor botanic pale ale

What you do

1. Using a large saucepan on medium heat, add the olive oil and onion. Cook for 5 minutes then add the garlic, paprika and cumin. Cook for a further minute then add the rest of the ingredients.
2. Bring to a boil, cover with a lid, then simmer for 35 minutes. Season to taste with ground sea salt and ground black pepper.

SHITAKE & BALSAMIC ROASTED TOMATO BRUSCHETTA WITH LAVENDER PESTO

What you need

For the bruschetta
1 French baguette, cut into 1inch rounds & toasted
150g shitake mushrooms, cut in half with stems discarded "use for a mushroom stock"
3 shallots, peeled and roughly chopped
150ml balsamic vinegar, such as aceto balsamico di modena
250g cherry tomatoes
150ml vegan white wine
2 tablespoons vegan butter
1 tablespoon sesame oil

For the lavender pesto
6 stalks of fresh lavender washed then the end flower piece cut into a fine powder.
80g fresh basil

3 tablespoons olive oil

5 tablespoons cold water

2 shallots, peeled and roughly chopped

6 cloves garlic, peeled and roughly chopped

4 tablespoons pine nuts toasted (if nut allergy, try sunflower seeds or pumpkin seeds, same amount)

1 lemon, juiced

3 tablespoons nutritional yeast

What you do

For the lavender pesto

1. Using a standing blender, add the basil, lavender, shallots, garlic, yeast and lemon juice.
2. Put the blender on a medium speed then puree the ingredients.
3. Slowly drizzle in the oil in a steady stream.
4. Add a touch of water if the sauce splits then blend.

For the bruschetta

1. Start off by roasting the tomatoes by preheating your oven to 190°c/375°f. Using a small baking tray, add the tomatoes and balsamic vinegar. Roast in the oven for roughly 25 minutes or until the tomatoes are charred and blistered. Take out and set aside.
2. Using a medium sized skillet on high heat, add the butter and sesame oil. When the oils are sizzling, add the mushrooms and shallots and season with a touch of ground sea salt and ground black pepper.
3. Continue cooking for roughly 5 minutes then add the white wine, when the wine has almost reduced, toss in the balsamic tomatoes then take the pan off the heat.

To assemble the bruschetta

Place the mushroom and tomato mixture onto a round of the baguette toast, then add a teaspoon of pesto on top.

POBLANO & SWEET POTATO NUT ROAST

This dish uses one of my favourite chillies, the mellow poblano! It is a very mild chilli but when you chargrill it, it gives off a sweet smoky depth of flavour.

What you need

*If you have a food processor this will work wonders for chopping the vegetables!

4 poblano peppers
1 medium sized red onion, peeled and finely chopped
1 medium sized sweet potato, peeled and cut into roughly 2cm size cubes
250ml oat milk
40g sage, roughly chopped
2 tablespoons marmite
5 cloves garlic, peeled and finely chopped
2 tablespoons tomato paste
100g cooked lentils
1 teaspoon ground sea salt
¼ teaspoon ground black pepper
80g regular mushrooms, finely chopped
70g walnuts, toasted and finely chopped
70g almonds, toasted and finely chopped
3 tablespoons ground flaxseed meal
140g panko breadcrumbs

What you do

Preparing the poblano chillies

1. Preheat your oven to 180°c/350°f then prepare your poblanos. Simply place all 4 poblanos on a gas flame and turn periodically until all sides of the peppers are thoroughly scorched and blackened. Place into a bowl and cover with cling film then set aside for 10 minutes.
2. Peel the poblanos, discard the seeds and then cut up the poblanos into a fine dice and set aside.

Preparing the nut roast

1. Using a large pot on medium heat, add a splash of olive oil then cook the onions until they start to turn brown, roughly 3 minutes. Then add the sweet potatoes, garlic and oat milk.
2. Cook for 15 minutes making sure to stir the bottom of the pot periodically, then add the mushrooms, nuts, lentils, tomato paste, marmite, sage, poblanos and salt and pepper.
3. Cook for a further 5 minutes then take off the heat. Mix in thoroughly the breadcrumbs and flaxseed meal.
4. Transfer the mixture to a 9inch by 5inch loaf tin lined with parchment paper and bake at 180°c/350°f for 70 minutes. Take out of the oven and let sit for 20 minutes to let the loaf slightly congeal.

MAC N CHEESE

What you need

For the pasta
300g macaroni pasta
350ml cashew cream - Page 52
2 tablespoons nutritional yeast flakes
1 teaspoon apple cider vinegar

For the cheese crust
3 tablespoons nutritional yeast flakes
4 tablespoons cashew nuts, roughly chopped
30g coconut oil, melted
320ml cashew cream
1 teaspoon onion powder
1 teaspoon smoked paprika

What you do

1. Cook off the macaroni in a medium sized pot of boiling water, drain then place into a large baking pan.
2. Mix in the cashew cream, yeast flakes and vinegar and set aside.
3. In a medium sized bowl, mix all the cheese crust ingredients, then evenly add onto the top of the pasta.
4. Bake at 180°c/350°f for 25 minutes or until its nice and golden brown.

CAJUN SUCCOTASH

What you need

10oz vegan bacon
1 small red onion, roughly chopped
4 garlic cloves, peeled and finely chopped
4 ears of corn, kernels cut off and cobs discarded
1 tablespoon apple cider vinegar
1 teaspoon smoked paprika
300ml vegetable stock
3 poblano chillies
300g isle of wight cherry tomatoes, left whole
60g basil, roughly chopped
2 jalapenos, finely chopped
1, 12oz can borlotti beans, drained
8oz okra, cut into ½ inch chunks

What you do

1. Start off by charring your poblanos on a naked medium flame, char all over until blackened and blistered. Place into a bowl and cover with cling film. Let sit for 10 minutes, deseed then peel peppers and roughly chop.
2. Using a large pot on medium heat, add a splash of olive oil then add the red onion and garlic. Cook for 2 minutes or until the garlic begins to brown, then add the vegetable stock, corn, bacon, tomatoes, vinegar, paprika, poblanos, jalapenos, and okra.
3. Bring the pot to a boil then simmer for 25 minutes making sure to stir the pot periodically to prevent scorching. After 25 minutes, add the borlotti beans & basil, cook for a further 5 minutes then serve.

CANNELINI BEAN & OLIVE HUMMUS WITH DUKKAH

What you need

For the hummus
150g canned chickpeas
150g canned cannellini beans

100g green olives, pitted
60ml extra virgin olive oil
5 garlic cloves, peeled and roughly chopped
1 lemon, juiced
3 tablespoons tahini paste
¾ teaspoon smoked paprika
½ teaspoon ground sea salt
Pinch of ground black pepper

For the dukkah
2 tablespoons coriander seeds
2 tablespoons fennel seeds
2 tablespoons cumin seeds
2 tablespoons sesame seeds
50g hazelnuts
50g almonds
½ teaspoon ground sea salt

What you do

For the hummus
1. Using a large food processor, add half of the olive oil and all the garlic. Puree until the garlic is finely chopped then add the chickpeas, cannellini beans, olives, lemon, tahini, paprika, salt & pepper.
2. Puree on high speed, drizzling in the rest of the oil. When all the oil is incorporated, you should have a nice thick hummus, if to thick, add some water and if to lose, add some more beans. Season to taste with ground sea salt and ground black pepper.

For the dukkah
1. Start off by preheating your oven to 180°c/350°f. Place all the ingredients onto a large baking tray lined with parchment paper and bake for roughly 10 minutes or until they are thoroughly toasted.

WILD MUSHROOMS OVER MARMITE UDON NOODLES

What you need

400g wild mushrooms, left whole
2 tablespoons olive oil
1 tablespoon vegan butter
100ml white wine
20g fresh sage, roughly chopped
3 shallots, peeled and thinly sliced
4 cloves garlic, peeled and thinly sliced
250g udon noodles
2 tablespoons marmite
400ml vegetable stock

What you do

For the mushrooms
1. Using a large sauté pan on high heat, add the olive oil and vegan butter, when sizzling add the shallots and mushrooms then cook for 2 minutes on the high heat.
2. Add the garlic and sage, when the garlic starts to brown, add the white wine. Cook for a further 2 minutes then season to taste and set aside.

For the udon noodles
1. Place the noodles in bowl then submerge in boiling water, let sit for 2 minutes.
2. Using a medium sized pot, add the vegetable stock & marmite. Bring to the boil, then add the strained noodles and simmer for 3 minutes. Pour the noodles into a bowl followed by the mushrooms on top.

PORTOBELLO PUPUSAS WITH PICKLED VEGETABLES

What you need

For the pupusas
2 cups maseca corn flour
1.5 cups warm water
¼ teaspoon fine sea salt
3 large portobello mushrooms, roughly chopped
3 shallots, peeled and roughly chopped
4 cloves garlic, peeled and sliced thinly
250g grated vegan cheese
1 teaspoon smoked paprika

For the pickled vegetables
2 medium sized carrots, peeled and cut into thin julienne
8 radishes, ends snipped off then cut into thin slices
100g white cabbage, cut into thin julienne
200ml water
200ml cider vinegar
100g brown sugar
2 teaspoons dried oregano
¼ teaspoon black onion seeds
1 tablespoon sea salt

What you do

For the pupusas
1. Using a medium sized bowl, pour in the maseca & salt, give a little mix then add half of the water. Mix in, then mix in the rest of the water, knead and mix in for roughly 2 minutes. If the dough seems a little dry, add a tablespoon of warm water. The dough should be a soft play-do like texture and not sticky. Cover and leave to rest for 20 minutes before using.
2. Using a large skillet on high heat, add a splash of olive oil then add the mushrooms, shallots, garlic and paprika. Cover with a lid and cook for 3 minutes stirring a couple of times, add the vegan cheese, sea salt and ground black pepper to taste.

3. To make the pupusas, take roughly a lemon sized piece of dough and flatten into a round pancake shape, using your fingers make an indentation in the middle then add 3 tablespoons of the mushroom filling. Fold the outside dough over the centre filling and flatten slightly into a pancake shape, roughly 1inch thick by 6inches round. Leave to chill in the fridge for 20 minutes.

For the pickled vegetables
1. Using a non-reactive sauce pot, add all the ingredients apart from the radishes. Bring the pot to a boil, then simmer for 4 minutes, add the radishes then pour into a warmed container with a close-fitting lid or glass jar.
2. When the ingredients are in the jar, close the lid then leave overnight to absorb the flavours. These pickled vegetables can be kept for up to 3 months either in the fridge or in a cool, dark area of your kitchen away from direct sunlight.

PAPPARDELLE PRIMAVERA WITH POMODORO SAUCE

What you need

2 servings of pappardelle pasta

For the primavera
1 medium sized courgette, roughly chopped
1 bell pepper, seeded and roughly chopped
2 shallots, peeled and roughly chopped
6 shitake mushrooms, stems discarded & roughly chopped "can use stems for a mushroom stock"
2 pak choi, thoroughly washed and roughly chopped
8 cherry tomatoes, cut in half
200ml vegetable stock
1 teaspoon ground sea salt
¼ teaspoon ground black pepper
1 tablespoon olive oil
1 tablespoon vegan butter

For the pomodoro sauce
3lb roma tomatoes, cored and ends scored with a paring knife
5 shallots, peeled and thinly sliced

12 cloves garlic, peeled and thinly sliced
200ml white wine
80g fresh basil, roughly chopped
2 tablespoons demerara sugar
1 tablespoon apple cider vinegar
1 teaspoon ground sea salt
½ teaspoon ground black pepper
1 tablespoon vegan butter

What you do

For the spaghetti
1. Using a medium sized pot, bring to boil 3 litres of water then add the pasta and a pinch of salt. Turn the heat down to a simmer and cook for 10 minutes, drain & mix with a splash of olive oil then set aside.

For the primavera
1. Using a large skillet on high heat, add the olive oil and vegan butter, wait until it is sizzling then add the shallots and mushrooms. Cook until the shallots start to turn brown then add everything else.
2. Cover with a lid, bring to a boil and simmer for 6 minutes. Set aside.

For the pomodoro sauce
Preparing the tomatoes
1. Using a large pot, bring some water to the boil and boil the tomatoes for 16 seconds only. Take out the tomatoes and place into a bowl of cold water with some ice. This stops the tomatoes from cooking.
2. Using a small paring knife, peel the skins off the tomatoes then give them a rough chop.

For the sauce
1. Using a large pot on medium heat, add the olive oil and vegan butter. When sizzling, add the shallots and garlic then cover with a lid.
2. After 2 minutes, add the remaining ingredients, bring to a boil then simmer for 35 minutes stirring periodically.

THREE BEAN CHILLI & JACKFRUIT

What you need

For the chilli
1 medium sized red onion, peeled and roughly chopped
6 cloves garlic, peeled and finely chopped
1 leek, washed and roughly chopped
1 12oz can jackfruit, roughly chopped
200g cooked kidney beans
200g cooked borlotti beans
2 tablespoons marmite
400g tinned chopped tomatoes
2 tablespoons tomato paste
600ml vegetable stock
2 tablespoons chilli powder
2 teaspoons dried oregano
2 teaspoons smoked paprika
2 teaspoons ground cumin

For the aubergine chips
1 small aubergine, all the skin peeled and cut into very thin strips
1 tablespoon flour
1 teaspoon smoked paprika
100ml canola or rapeseed oil

What you do

For the chilli
1. Using a large saucepan on medium heat, add the olive oil and vegan butter, when nice and sizzling, add the onions, garlic and all the spices. Cover with a lid and let cook for 2 minutes.
2. Add the remaining ingredients, bring to a boil then simmer for 40 minutes, stirring periodically.

For the aubergine chips
1. Using a small skillet, heat up the canola or rapeseed oil to 160°c/320°f.
2. Toss the aubergine chips into a bowl with the flour and smoked paprika, dredge to shake off surplus flour then shallow fry in batches for 14 seconds at a time. Drain onto paper towels and sprinkle with a little ground sea salt.

KOHLRABI & JACKFRUIT TACO WITH JALAPENO CREAM

What you need

1 small kohlrabi, thinly sliced
1 handful of pea shoots
1 12oz tin jackfruit, drained
1 small red onion, finely chopped
2 medium sized tomatoes, finely chopped
1 avocado, cut into small pieces
200ml jalapeno cream "recipe on page 39"

What you do

1. Using a medium sized bowl, toss together the jackfruit, onions, tomatoes & jalapeno cream. Season with a touch of sea salt and ground black pepper.
2. Lay out the kohlrabi discs and place 2 tablespoons of the filling into each disc, followed by the pea shoots. Serve as they are onto platters or for a smooth looking taco, fold up and clip with a mini clothes peg.

ROOT VEGETABLE VINDALOO CURRY

What you need

1 medium sized onion, roughly chopped
5 garlic cloves, finely chopped
1 small swede, cut into roughly 1cm cubes
1 small turnip, cut into roughly 1cm cubes
2 carrots, cut into roughly 1cm cubes
1 small kohlrabi, cut into roughly 1cm cubes
1 12oz tin chopped tomatoes
200ml jalapeno cream
6 tomatoes, cored and roughly chopped
1 teaspoon whole black peppercorns
1 teaspoon mustard seeds
1 teaspoon cumin seeds

1 teaspoon cardamom seeds
1 teaspoon ground turmeric
1 tablespoon brown sugar
1 habanero pepper, finely chopped
1 thumb sized piece of ginger, grated
2 teaspoons garam masala
2 jalapenos, roughly chopped
100ml apple cider vinegar

What you do

For the marinade

1. Using a cast iron skillet or non-stick sauté pan on medium heat, add the peppercorns, mustard seeds, cumin seeds and cardamom seeds. Toast lightly until all slightly brown or toasted all over, roughly 1 minute. Transfer to a spice grinder and blend until of a powdery substance.
2. Add these spices to a bowl then add the following, ground turmeric, sugar, ginger, garam masala & vinegar. Mix the ingredients together then set aside.
3. Using a large sauté pan on medium heat, add a good glug of olive oil then add the onions and garlic. Let cook for 4 minutes then add the bowl of spices. Keep cooking for a further 2 minutes, then add the rest of the ingredients and bring to a boil.
4. Transfer to a large roasting pan and cover with foil, bake at 170°c for 40 minutes, take off the foil and stir, then continue cooking for 20 minutes. I like to serve this with jasmine rice, adding a stick of lemongrass to the cooking water for a nice infusion.

SWEET POTATO THAI CURRY

What you need

1 tablespoon coconut oil
1 red onion, peeled and roughly chopped
A thumb sized piece of ginger, peeled and minced
5 garlic cloves, grated
2 tablespoons Thai red curry paste
600g sweet potato, peeled and cut into bite size chunks
400ml coconut milk
200ml cashew cream, page 52
1 lemongrass stick, cut in half
1 lime, cut in half
300g chard, stem discarded and chopped into bite sized pieces

What you do

1. Using a large saucepan on medium heat, add the coconut oil and onions, cook for 4 minutes then add the garlic & ginger. Mix in for a minute then add the thai curry paste.
2. Thoroughly mix in the curry paste, squeeze out the lime juice into the pot and put the 2 lime halves in there also. Add the remaining ingredients, cover with a lid and simmer for 35 minutes stirring periodically. Season to taste with sea salt and ground black pepper.

JACKFRUIT BRUSCHETTA

What you need

1 small butternut squash, peeled and cut into a small dice
0.5 tablespoon brown sugar
6oz canned jackfruit, drained and cut into bite size pieces
10 cherry tomatoes, red & yellow cut into quarters
3 tablespoons of chives, finely sliced
1 tablespoon pine nuts
100g vegan cheese, cut into a small dice
2 slices of thick artisanal bread, toasted. In picture is a wholemeal and rye bread from Cantina's.
Small handful of pea shoots
2 tablespoons oil of wight

What you do

1. Using a sauté pan on medium heat, add one tablespoon of the olive oil, the butternut squash and the brown sugar. When the squash starts to brown and caramelize, add 350ml of water, give a little stir then boil until all the moisture has evaporated. You will be left with a nice slightly caramelized squash puree. Season to taste with sea salt and ground black pepper.
2. Using a medium sized bowl, combine the jackfruit, tomatoes, pine nuts, cheese & chives. Dress with a splash of oil of wight then place onto a toasted piece of rustic bread. Bake in the oven at 200°c/400°f for 10 minutes to slightly melt the cheese and serve with the pea shoots drizzled with a splash of oil of wight.

BEETROOT CAPONATA OVER BRAISED CELERIAC

What you need

For the caponata
400g beetroot, peeled and cut into roughly 2cm cubes
2 aubergines, cut into roughly 2cm cubes
2 12oz cans plum tomatoes
1 red onion, peeled and finely chopped
50ml red wine vinegar
100ml olive oil
3 tablespoons capers
60g raisins
50g parsley, roughly chopped
1 jalapeno, stem discarded and roughly chopped

For the celeriac
1 celeriac, peeled and sliced into 1inch thick rounds
300ml vegetable stock
1 tablespoon chopped rosemary

What you do

For the caponata
1. Using a large skillet on medium heat, add the oil and when hot, add the aubergine. Cook for roughly 20 minutes then take out of the oil and set aside.
2. Add the onions and cook until they start to brown, then add the rest of the ingredients including the aubergines. Cover with a lid and simmer for 40 minutes.

For the celeriac
1. Using a roasting pan, add the sliced celeriac, vegetable stock and rosemary. Cover with foil then bake for 25 minutes at 180°c/350°f. Add the celeriac to a round bowl, then place the caponata on top.

VEGAN MEATBALLS IN FRA DIAVOLO TOMATO SAUCE

What you need

For the meatballs
2 tablespoons olive oil
1 red onion, finely chopped
50g portobella mushrooms, finely chopped
4 garlic cloves, finely chopped
1 teaspoon smoked paprika
1 teaspoon dried oregano
1, 12oz can borlotti beans, drained
80g rolled oats
50g breadcrumbs

For the spicy tomato sauce
2 tablespoons olive oil
5 shallots, finely chopped
4 garlic cloves, finely chopped
1 teaspoon dried chilli flakes
1 jalapeno, finely sliced
2 x 400g cans chopped tomatoes
1 tablespoon brown sugar
50g basil, roughly chopped
1 teaspoon dried oregano
1 tablespoon marmite

What you do

For the sauce
1. Using a medium sized saucepan on medium heat, add the olive oil and shallots, cook for roughly 3 minutes then add the garlic.
2. When the garlic starts to brown, add the jalapeno, chilli flakes, marmite, oregano, tomatoes, sugar and basil.
3. Bring to a boil then simmer for 20 minutes. Season to taste with ground sea salt and ground black pepper.

For the meatballs

1. Start off by preparing your binding ingredient which helps the meatballs stay together "this is the borlotti beans, oats and breadcrumbs".
2. Place the beans, oats and breadcrumbs into a food processor and blitz until all chopped and combined then set aside.
3. Using a large sauté pan on high heat, add the 2 tablespoons of olive oil, onions, mushrooms, garlic, paprika and oregano.

Cook down for 10 minutes or until most of the moisture has evaporated. Mix this with the bean mixture and season with a touch of ground sea salt and ground black pepper. Shape the meatballs into 3oz balls then place onto a tray and chill for 20 minutes. Using a large sauté pan on high heat, add a splash of olive oil then the meatballs, brown on both sides then add the tomato sauce, add enough sauce so it comes up to halfway of the meatballs, along with 200ml of water. Cover and bake at 180°c/350°f for 25 minutes then serve.

VEGETABLE STOCK

6 litres cold water
2 large carrots, peeled and roughly chopped
2 large white onions, peeled and roughly chopped
1 head of celery, washed and roughly chopped
10 black peppercorns
6 bay leaves
1 head of garlic, cut in half
100g fresh parsley
100g fresh thyme

1. Place all the ingredients into a large pot then bring to a boil, then turndown to a simmer.
2. Using a ladle, periodically skim the surface impurities off and discard, simmer for 2 hours then strain through a muslin cloth. Let cool slightly before placing into the fridge.

DESSERTS

COCONUT CORNBREAD

What you need

For the coconut cornbread
200g yellow cornmeal
80g shredded coconut
1 teaspoon baking powder
170g self raising flour
1 teaspoon baking soda
0.5 teaspoon ground sea salt
260ml almond milk
120g vegan butter
100g brown sugar
5 tablespoons coconut oil
Cashew ice cream – recipe on page 66
Chocolate shards – recipe on page 46

What you do

1. Preheat your oven to 200°c/400°f and grease a 9x9 inch baking tray with the vegan butter. Into a mixing bowl, add the cornmeal, flour, baking powder, baking soda and salt.
2. Using a small saucepan, melt the vegan butter then add the brown sugar and mix in until dissolved, take off the heat then add the cornmeal mixture and almond milk. Bake for 25 minutes or until you insert a knife and it comes out clean, and hot.

MATCHA & POPPY SEED MADELINE'S

What you need

80g vegan butter, melted
100g sugar
120g self-raising flour
1 teaspoon baking powder
2 tablespoons vegan egg replacer
2 tablespoons matcha powder
2 tablespoons coconut oil
1 tablespoon poppy seeds
100ml almond milk
Pinch of ground sea salt
1 teaspoon vanilla extract

What you do

For the madeleine batter

1. Using a large mixing bowl, mix in the flour, sugar, baking powder, poppy seeds, salt and matcha powder.
2. In a separate small bowl, mix the following - almond milk, egg replacer and vanilla extract. Add this mixture to the matcha mix and stir with a wooden spoon or a rubber spatula. Add half of the vegan butter to this mixture, when combined, add the rest of the butter and coconut oil. Cover the bowl with cling film and leave to rest in the fridge overnight or at least 5 hours.

Cooking the madeleines

1. Preheat your oven to 190°c/375°f. Using madeleine moulds, drizzle a little olive oil into the moulds then rub the oil inside the moulds with your fingers. Take out the madeleine batter and fill each mould with 1 tablespoon of the madeleine batter and bake for 12 minutes.
2. Leave them to rest for 5 minutes before taking them out of their moulds, then sprinkle with powdered sugar.

HABANERO HOT CHOCOLATE

What you need

1 habanero, stem discarded, and cut in half
3 tablespoons cocoa powder
300ml almond milk
30g cashew nuts
30g vegan dark chocolate, broken into small pieces
½ teaspoon vanilla extract
Pinch of ground sea salt

What you do

1. Using a medium sized saucepan, add the habanero, cocoa powder, vanilla extract, cashew nuts, sea salt and almond milk. Place onto a low heat and bring to a simmer, keep simmering for 5 minutes then take off the heat.
2. Add the vegan dark chocolate and mix in until it has melted. Place the hot chocolate into a standing blender, start on slow speed then gear up to high speed, blitz on high speed for 1 minute. Strain through a muslin cloth and serve.

LEMON & HIBISCUS LOAF CAKE

What you need

For the cake
 320g self raising flour
280g granulated sugar
2 teaspoons baking soda
½ teaspoon ground fine sea salt
340ml almond milk
100ml extra virgin olive oil
1 teaspoon vanilla extract
Juice of 2 lemons, plus both lemons zested
10 hibiscus flowers, finely chopped

For the lemon frosting
500g powdered sugar

100g vegan butter
Juice of two lemons

What you do

For the cake
1. Preheat the oven to 180°c/350°f. Grease 2 loaf tin pans with a touch of vegan butter and set aside.
2. Using a large mixing bowl, add the sugar, baking soda, salt and flour, give a little mix then add the almond milk, olive oil, vinegar, vanilla and lemon juice.
3. Mix until combined and no lumps are visible. Pour into the loaf tins and bake for 30 minutes or until you insert a knife into the centre and it comes out clean and hot. Take out of the oven, let sit for 10 minutes then take out of the tin and leave to cool completely before adding the frosting.

For the frosting
1. Put the powdered sugar, vegan butter and lemon juice into your electric mixing bowl.
2. Start off slowly to fully mix, then gradually increase the speed until the mixture is smooth and thick.

CARROT & CASHEW CAKE

What you need

For the cake
80g cashew nuts, toasted & roughly chopped
5 carrots, peeled & grated
1 teaspoon ground nutmeg
1 orange, zested
1 teaspoon ground ginger
1 teaspoon baking soda
1 teaspoon baking powder
2 tablespoons flaxseed meal, mixed with 5 tablespoons water
400g self raising flour
200ml oat milk
1 teaspoon vanilla extract
280g brown sugar
250ml coconut oil

For the frosting

4 tablespoons vegan butter
470g powdered sugar
½ cup cashew nuts, toasted and finely chopped
1 teaspoon vanilla extract

What you do

For the cake

1. Preheat the oven to 180°c/350°f, then liberally grease two round cake tins.
2. Using a large bowl, add the baking soda, salt, baking powder, flour, nutmeg, carrot and sugar and give a little mix.
3. In a separate small bowl, add the flaxseed and water then leave to sit for roughly 40 seconds. Add the vanilla, oil, cashew nuts and flaxseed mixture to the flour mixture.
4. Mix thoroughly, you should have a batter that when you drop some off a spoon it will slowly slide off. If too thick, add some more oat milk, too wet, add some flour.
5. Bake for 30 minutes or until you insert a knife and the knife comes out clean and hot. Leave to cool completely before adding the frosting.

For the frosting

1. Using an electric mixing bowl, add the vegan butter, powdered sugar and vanilla. Mix on slow speed to start then gradually speed up until thoroughly combined then add the cashew nuts.
2. Spread half of this frosting onto the top layer of a chilled sponge round, then lay the other round on top. Garnish with the leftover frosting

RHUBARB & LAVENDER PANNA COTTA

What you need

400g fresh rhubarb stalks, washed and chopped into 2inch pieces
10 fresh lavender whole stalks with flower
1 lime, cut into wedges
1 lemon, cut into wedges
8 cardamom seeds
2 litres almond milk
60g sugar plus 2 teaspoon agar agar powder

What you do

1. Add the almond milk, sugar and agar to a medium sized saucepan and stir well.
2. Then add the rhubarb, lavender, lime, lemon & cardamom. Mix well, then bring to a boil and simmer for 3 minutes stirring all the time.
3. Take off the heat then strain though a fine strainer or muslin cloth into a container. Pour the mixture into dessert bowls and chill for at least 6 hours.

RUM HORCHATA

What you need

150ml rum
100g sugar
40g sliced almonds
400ml cold water
2 teaspoons vanilla extract
2 cinnamon sticks
450ml almond milk
220g long grain white rice

What you do

1. Place all the ingredients apart from the water into a standing blender, blend on high speed for 20 seconds. Scrape down the sides of the blender then blend again on high speed for 40 seconds.
2. Pour this mixture into a bowl then stir in the water, let marinate overnight in the fridge.
3. Strain the horchata through a cheese cloth and serve chilled in a glass over crushed ice, garnish with a cinnamon stick.

VANILLA & CASHEW ICE CREAM

What you need

75g cashew nuts
70ml water
4 tablespoons cocoa butter
4 tablespoons coconut oil
1 teaspoon ground sea salt
230ml coconut milk
2 teaspoons vanilla extract

What you do

1. Soak the cashew nuts in a bowl of water overnight then put the bowl of an ice cream machine in the freezer overnight to chill.
2. On the next day, add the cashews and soaking water to a standing blender, blend on high speed for 50 seconds. Strain into a bowl using a fine sieve.
3. Using a small saucepan over medium heat, add the water and sugar. Cook for roughly 2 minutes, stirring consistently. Then whisk in the cocoa butter, coconut oil and salt, remove from the heat and set aside. Using a standing blender, add the cashew milk and coconut milk, blend on medium speed and with the motor on, pour in the sugar then continue to blend for a further 90 seconds.
4. Pour this mixture into a large bowl and mix in the vanilla extract, have this chill for around an hour then add to the ice cream machine and churn for 50 minutes. Transfer the cream to a pan and freeze overnight.

EUCALYPTUS POACHED PEAR
& SUNFLOWER SEED GRANOLA

What you need

For the eucalyptus poached pear
2 pears such as conference or William's, peeled with stalk left on
6 eucalyptus leaves
350ml white wine
400ml water
2 tablespoons maple syrup

1 prickly pear, cut into thin wedges

For the sunflower seed granola
1 tablespoons sunflower seeds
1 tablespoon pumpkin seeds
100g whole rolled oats
40g sliced almonds
4 tablespoons shredded coconut
4 tablespoons coconut oil
2 tablespoons maple syrup
Pinch of fine sea salt

What you do

For the eucalyptus poached pear
1. Place all the ingredients into a baking dish and cover with aluminium foil.
2. Bake at 160°c/320°f for 30 minutes. Take out of the oven and discard the foil.
Pour the remaining liquid into a small saucepan, reduce on a low heat until you have roughly 1 cup of liquid left and pour back into the dish of pears.

Sunflower and pumpkin seed granola
Mix all the items together and place onto a baking tray, bake at 160°c/320°f for 25 minutes.

DRIMYS WINTERI SPICED CAKE

What you need

For the Cake
2 tablespoons pumpkin seeds, toasted
1 tablespoon sunflower seeds, toasted
125g phase vegan butter, melted
125g soft brown sugar
1 teaspoon baking powder
150ml oat milk
250g self-rising flour
2 teaspoons winter bark spice
3 tablespoons coconut oil

For the Icing
1 tablespoon pumpkin seeds, toasted 1
tablespoon sunflower seeds, toasted
40g cashew nuts, toasted and finely chopped 60ml
almond milk, warm
900g icing sugar

What you do

For the icing
Mix all the ingredients together, add more milk if needed to get a thick gluey type consistency.

For the cake
1. Preheat the oven to 175°c/350°f then line a cake tin with the vegan butter.

2. Place all the cake ingredients into a bowl then mix until all fully combined.

3. Place into the cake tin then bake for 30 minutes or until you insert a toothpick and it comes out clean and hot. Place on a cooling rack to let cool completely before icing the cake.

BITS N BOBS

MARINARA SAUCE

6 tablespoons extra virgin olive oil

3 shallots, peeled and finely chopped

6 cloves garlic, peeled and sliced thinly

1 35oz can of san Marzano tomatoes, slightly crushed by hand

40g basil, roughly chopped

1. Using a large cast iron skillet or sauté pan on medium heat, add the olive oil, shallots and garlic. Stirring frequently cook until the garlic is browned then add the tomatoes and a touch of sea salt and black pepper.

2. Simmer for 30 minutes, periodically stirring the bottom of the pan making sure it doesn't burn then add the basil towards the last 5 minutes of cooking then season to taste.

BALSAMIC ONION & OLIVE RELISH

4 large red onions, cut into julienne
300g kalamata olives, pitted and roughly chopped
120g white sugar
2 tablespoons black onion seeds
400ml balsamic vinegar

1. Using a medium sized pot on medium heat, add all the ingredients and bring to a boil.
2. Turn down the heat to a low simmer and cook for roughly 2 hours or until the relish is of a nice thick consistency. Periodically stir the relish making sure it doesn't stick to the bottom of the pot.

ORANGE & CARDAMOM MARMALADE

14 oranges
12 cardamom pods, wrapped in cheesecloth and tied together with string
 5 cups white sugar

1. Using a large pot, clip a sugar thermometer onto the inside of your saucepan, then add the oranges and cover with water making sure the oranges are submerged. Bring to the boil and cook for around 30 minutes or until you can pierce the skin with your fingertips with ease.
2. Take out the oranges and set aside, discard half the water and keep the rest of the water in the pot.
3. Cut the oranges in half, scrape out all the pulp with a spoon and give a rough chop, add this pulp back to the pot of orange stock. Now, slice half of the orange skins into ½ cm thick slices and add to the orange stock along with the cardamom pod bag.
4. Simmer the marmalade until it reaches the setting point which will be 105°c/220°f.

BALSAMIC ROASTED TOMATOES

With the natural caramelisation of tomato and balsamic roasted together, these little beauties are one of my favourites. I try to add these little beauties to as many dishes as I can, such as salads, sandwiches and bruschetta's.

What you need

500g cherry tomatoes, such as isle of wight or heritage
100ml balsamic vinegar, such as Aceto balsamico di Modena or 25-year aged Ponte Vecchio balsamic
1 teaspoon olive oil
1 teaspoon sea salt
0.5 teaspoon ground black pepper

What you do

1. Using a small mixing bowl, add all the ingredients and mix well.
2. Lay out onto a baking tray lined with parchment paper then bake at 180°c/350°f for roughly 30 minutes or until the tomatoes have blistered and are slightly blackened.

PICKLED ROOT VEGETABLES

What you need

3 carrots, peeled and cut into large matchsticks
4 parsnips, peeled and cut into large matchsticks
1 celeriac, peeled and cut into large matchsticks
2 raw beetroots, peeled and cut into large matchsticks
1 jalapeno, thinly sliced
1 tablespoon cardamom seeds
1 tablespoon coriander seeds
3 teaspoons fennel seeds
1 teaspoon mustard seeds
1 teaspoon whole cloves
3 star anise
1 lime, cut into 4 wedges
4 cups cider vinegar
4 cups water
2 tablespoons sea salt
5 tablespoons sugar
"1 large mason jar for storage" clean and dry

What you do

1. Using a large saucepan, add all the ingredients then bring to the boil, simmer for 2 minutes then take off the heat.
2. Arrange the contents into your clean hot mason jars. Close the lid "it should be a tight-fitting lid", let cool to room temperature then leave to marinate. These can be kept for up to 3 weeks in the fridge.

CRANBERRY & QUINCE SAUCE

What you need

400g fresh cranberries
3 fresh quinces, cored and cut into a small dice
260g sugar
1 stick of cinnamon
1 star anise
1 orange, zested and juiced

200ml water
200ml tipsy wight quince vodka
0.5 teaspoon of sea salt

What you do

1. Using a medium sized saucepan on medium heat, add all the ingredients.
2. Bring to a boil then simmer for 30 minutes.

CHIMICHURRI

What you need

6 shallots, finely chopped
1 whole head of garlic, peeled and finely chopped
3 jalapenos, stems discarded and finely chopped
1 handful of chopped fresh parsley
1 handful of chopped coriander
1 teaspoon dried oregano
1 lemon, juiced
230ml extra virgin olive oil
4 tablespoons red wine vinegar
1 teaspoon ground sea salt
0.5 teaspoon ground black pepper

What you do

1. Add all the ingredients together then let marinate overnight. Use as a dressing for many dishes such as all meats and even salads.

CASHEW CREAM

What you need

150g cashew nuts, toasted
400ml soy milk

What you do

1. Soak the cashew nuts in the soy milk overnight in the fridge.
2. Bring to a boil then simmer for 10 minutes, puree in a standing blender on high speed for 30 seconds then strain.

ALMOND CREAM

What you need

150g almonds, toasted
400ml almond milk

What you do

1. Soak the almons in the soy milk overnight in the fridge.
2. Bring to a boil then simmer for 10 minutes, puree in a standing blender on high speed for 30 seconds then strain.

WALNUT & MAPLE CREAM

What you need

150g walnuts, toasted
400ml soy milk
3 tablespoons maple syrup

What you do

1. Soak the walnuts in the soy milk overnight in the fridge.
2. Bring to a boil with the maple syrup then simmer for 10 minutes, puree in a standing blender on high speed for 30 seconds then strain.

JALAPENO CREAM

What you need

5 jalapenos, stems discarded, and jalapenos roughly chopped
5 shallots, peeled and roughly chopped
400ml oat milk

What you do

1. Using a medium sized pot, bring all the ingredients to a boil, then simmer for 10 minutes.
2. Using a standing blender, puree on high speed for 30 seconds then strain.

CURRY SALT

What you need

1 tablespoon cumin seeds
1 tablespoon coriander seeds
1 tablespoon cardamom seeds
6 tablespoons wight sea salt
1 teaspoon ground turmeric
1 teaspoon fenugreek
1 teaspoon ground ginger
½ tablespoon fennel seeds
1 teaspoon garlic powder
½ tcaspoon chilli powder
1 teaspoon smoked paprika

What you do

1. Using a medium sized skillet on medium heat, add the cumin, coriander, cardamom & fennel seeds. Toast until the seeds just start to brown then pour into a mortar and pestle or spice grinder.
2. Let the seeds cool down for 10 minutes then grind into a powder, once finely ground, add the remaining ingredients and grind to combine all the items.

JALAPENO SMOKED SALT

What you need

5 jalapenos, stems cut off and discarded
8 tablespoons Maldon smoked sea salt

What you do

1. Cut the jalapenos in half lengthways then cut into roughly 1inch pieces.
2. Place the chillies in a dehydrator along with the seeds and dehydrate overnight on your highest setting, if you do not have a dehydrator, bake them in the oven at 110°c/230°f for roughly 3 hours or until they are crisp to the touch.
3. Leave them to cool down then grind in a mortar and pestle or spice grinder, once finely ground add the salt and combine.

BLUEBERRY ROOIBOS & LEMON TEA

What you need

1 tablespoon blueberry rooibos loose leaf tea leaves
1 teaspoon brown sugar
1 lemon wedge
200ml cold water

What you do

1. Bring all the ingredients to a boil, then cover and let steep for 4 minutes.
2. Strain through a tea strainer and serve.

TURMERIC & CRANBERRY TEA

What you need

2 green tea sachets
200g fresh cranberries, rinsed
60g fresh turmeric root, peeled and sliced as thin as you can
80g demerara sugar
500ml cold water

What you do

1. Place all the ingredients into a medium sized non-reactive pot and bring to a simmer with the lid on.
2. Simmer for 2 minutes then take off the heat. Discard the tea bags then using a hand-held blender, puree slightly to help break down the cranberries.
3. Strain the liquid through a muslin cloth then chill in the fridge with the lid on. This tea can be served hot or even chilled over some ice.

CISTUSINCANUS GREEN TEA

"Apparently, cistusincanus is known for treating Influenza A"

What you need

Two handfuls of cistus flowers and leaves
2 green tea, tea bags
1 teaspoon of fresh lemon juice
1 teaspoon demerara sugar

What you do

1. Leave the cistus flowers to air dry for 5 days or dehydrate overnight in a dehydrator on medium setting.
2. Place the dehydrated cistus leaves in a tea strainer and place into a container, along with the green tea bags, sugar and lemon juice. Pour over 400ml of boiling water and let steep for 4 minutes.

LAVENDER PESTO

What you need

100g basil leaves
100g lavender flowers
30g pine nuts
60ml water
½ teaspoon ground sea salt
¼ teaspoon ground black pepper
40ml fresh lemon juice
5 cloves garlic, peeled
10g nutritional yeast
40ml extra virgin olive oil

What you do

1. Place everything apart from the olive oil and water into a standing blender, pulse blend to mix all the ingredients.
2. Keeping the blender on medium speed, in a slow but steady stream add all the olive oil, if it is too thick, add some water to get a smooth thick paste.

PUMPKIN RELISH

What you need

1 small pumpkin, peeled deseeded and cut into small chunks "roughly 2cm pieces"
1 small red onion, finely chopped
2 bay leaves
1 tablespoon fresh ginger, peeled and finely chopped
1 star anise
300ml water
3 tablespoons apple cider vinegar
2 tablespoons light brown sugar
2 garlic cloves, finely chopped
1 teaspoon sea salt

What you do

1. Using a medium sized pot on medium heat. Add a drizzle of olive oil and add the onion, garlic and ginger. Cook until the garlic starts to brown then add the rest of the ingredients.
2. Bring to a boil then simmer for roughly 30 minutes or until you have a nice thick relish. To test if thick enough, dip a tablespoon into the liquid, then run the tip of your finger in a line across the spoon, if the sauce does not run down, its ready. Season to taste.

CHILLI SIN CARNE

What you need

2 tablespoons olive oil
2 white onions, roughly chopped
5 garlic cloves, finely chopped
1 green bell pepper, roughly chopped
1 red bell pepper, roughly chopped
1 yellow bell pepper, roughly chopped
1 jalapeno, finely sliced
1 teaspoon ground coriander
1 teaspoon ground cumin
2 teaspoons dried oregano
2 tablespoons tomato puree
2 x 400g cans chopped tomatoes
250ml vegetable stock
2 tablespoons marmite
300g vegan mince
200g kidney beans
200g borlotti beans
2 teaspoons smoked paprika
200ml soy milk

What you do

1. Using a large saucepan on medium heat, add the olive oil, onions, coriander, cumin, paprika, garlic, peppers, and jalapeno.
2. Cook for 10 minutes with a lid on stirring periodically, then add all the other ingredients.
3. Bring to a boil then simmer for 30 minutes, stirring now and then to prevent scorching.

HALLOUMI & SWEET CHILLI KEBABS

What you need

225g halloumi, cut into bite size chunks
250g cherry tomatoes
250ml sweet chilli sauce
1 teaspoon minced ginger
120ml mango juice
3 spring onions, finely sliced
40g coriander leaf, finely chopped
14 10inch wooden kebab skewers

What you do

1. In a medium sized bowl mix together the chilli sauce, ginger, mango juice, onions and coriander.
2. Using wooden skewers, arrange the halloumi and tomatoes onto them alternating with each item. Lay out onto a tray then ladle the marinade over the skewers. Turn over to coat both sides.
3. Using a hot greased chargrill or bbq, grill the skewers on both sides for 2 minutes each and serve.

PINEAPPLE AND LYCHEE KEBABS WITH MERMAID GIN GLAZE

What you need

1 pineapple, cored and cut into bite size pieces
500g lychees, peeled
230ml mermaid gin
1 teaspoon brown sugar
1 star anise
2 tablespoons mint, finely chopped
14 wooden kebab skewers

What you do

1. Arrange the pineapple and lychees onto the skewers then arrange onto a platter and set aside.
2. Using a small saucepan, boil together the sugar, gin, mint & star anise. After it has come to the boil, turn down the heat and simmer for 10 minutes.
3. Spoon the warm gin mixture over the kebabs and serve.

ROOIBOS NEEDLE TEA FRUIT CAKE

What you need

220g dark brown sugar
200g vegan margarine
800g dried mixed fruit
1 lemon, grated
2 tablespoons coconut oil
3 tablespoons sunflower seeds
3 tablespoons linseed
240g gluten free self raising flour
0.5 teaspoon baking powder
1 tablespoon poppy seeds
3 tablespoons dark rum
4 teaspoons wight label rooibos tea leaves
150ml boiling water

What you do

1. Pour the boiling water over the rooibos tea in a small bowl, cover with cling film then let sit for 10 minutes.
2. Strain out the tea into a medium sized bowl then add the mixed fruit & linseed, let this marinate for 3 hours.
3. Preheat your oven to 160°c/320°f then grease a baking tin, roughly an 8inch baking tin. Whisk together the sugar and vegan margarine for roughly 4 minutes or until it seems to be a whiter colour.
4. Into another medium sized bowl, mix the flour, grated lemon, coconut oil, sunflower seeds & poppy seeds. Mix this into the mixed fruit mixture.
5. Place into the greased tin and bake for two hours. Enjoy with a cup of rooibos!

BACON & KOHLRABI BAO BUN

What you need

For the bacon
5 tablespoons soy sauce
3 tablespoons olive oil
3 tablespoons nutritional yeast flakes
1 teaspoon marmite
12 pieces of rice paper
2 teaspoons smoked paprika
2 tablespoons maple syrup
0.5 teaspoon ground black pepper
1 tablespoon barbecue sauce

For the filling
12 store bought bao buns
1 kohlrabi, peeled and finely chopped
1 teaspoon black onion seeds
2 tablespoons chimichurri

What you do

For the bacon
1. Preheat your oven to 180°c/350°f, then prepare the bacon.
2. Using a small bowl, mix everything together apart from the rice paper, this will be your bacon magic!
3. Lay out the rice paper sheets with one piece of rice paper on top of the other "6 stacks". Dip the rice papers into a bowl of water to help them soften slightly then cut into 3cm strips using sharp scissors or a very sharp knife.
4. Slide each rice paper strip into the marinade and onto the parchment paper, double check if the rice papers are all covered with the marinade then bake for 6 minutes. Check for crispiness if you want them crispier just cook them slightly longer. When slightly chilled, cut up into roughly 2cm size pieces.

Assembling the bao bun
1. Using a medium sized bowl, mix the kohlrabi, chimichurri and black onion seeds together then season to taste with ground sea salt and ground black pepper.

2. Add the bacon to the kohlrabi mixture then fill into your warmed bao buns.

CHOCOLATE SHARDS

What you need

140g cacao butter
120ml maple syrup
100g cocoa powder
50g tahini
2 teaspoons vanilla extract
0.5 teaspoon ground sea salt

What you do

1. Using a double boiler with a bowl sitting over a pot of simmering water, add the cacao butter and let it melt, stirring frequently.
2. As soon as it is melted, take it off the heat then add the maple syrup, vanilla, tahini and cocoa powder. Mix well, then spread the mixture out onto a large baking tray, place in the fridge for 3 hours until set. Break off shards when needed.

Printed in Great Britain
by Amazon